To:

_____

From:

_____

You're Invited
To Begin Your Easter At:

_____

Let every man and woman count himself immortal. Let him catch the revelation of Jesus in his resurrection. Let him say not merely, "Christ is risen," but "I shall rise."

Phillips Brooks

The Hope of Easter
Copyright © 2011 by Outreach Publishing

All rights reserved. No part of this book may be used or reproduced in any form or by any electronic or mechanical means including information storage and retrieval systems without permission from the author, except by a reviewer who may quote brief passages in a review.

Outreach, Inc., Vista, CA 92081
www.outreach.com

Scripture quotations from THE MESSAGE. Copyright © by Eugene H. Peterson 1993, 1994, 1995, 1996, 2000, 2001, 2002. Used by permission of NavPress Publishing Group.
Scripture quotations from the NEW AMERICAN STANDARD BIBLE®, Copyright © 1960, 1962, 1963, 1968, 1971, 1972, 1973, 1975, 1977, 1995 by The Lockman Foundation. Used by permission. Scripture quotations from The Holy Bible, New International Version® (NIV)®, copyright © 1973, 1978, 1984 by International Bible Society. Used by permission of Zondervan. All rights reserved. Scripture quotations from the Holy Bible, New Living Translation, copyright © 1996. Used by permission of Tyndale House Publishers, Inc., Wheaton, Illinois 60189. All rights reserved. Scripture quotations marked NKJV are taken from the New King James Version®. Copyright © 1982 by Thomas Nelson, Inc. Used by permission. All rights reserved. Scripture quotations marked NCV are taken from the New Century Version of the Bible, copyright © 2005 by Thomas Nelson, Inc. Used by permission. Scripture quotations marked NRSV are taken from the New Revised Standard Version Bible, copyright 1989, Division of Christian Education of the National Council of the Churches of Christ in the United States of America. Used by permission. All rights reserved.

ISBN: 978-1-9355-4134-9

Writing by Rebecca Currington in association with Snapdragon Group, Tulsa, OK, USA.
Cover and Interior Design: Tim Downs
Printed in the United States of America

Dear Friend,

You've been given this booklet as an invitation to a very special church service—an Easter celebration! It is a time when we come together to remember the resurrection of Jesus Christ, our Savior and King. The God we serve is unique. Though Jesus died a terrible death on the cross, there is no burial tomb, for the bonds of death could not hold Him. After three days, an angel pushed back the huge rock the Romans used to seal the tomb in which Jesus had been laid to rest. The living, resurrected Jesus then showed Himself to His disciples and ate breakfast with them around a campfire. He walked with them along the shore of the Sea of Galilee. He visited them where they were gathered together in secret. With others looking on, Jesus even urged Thomas, one of His disciples, to touch His hands and His side to prove that He was truly their Jesus, alive again.

For us, the resurrection of Jesus Christ holds ultimate significance. Because He was raised, from the dead, we can trust that we will be raised, as well. Because of His blameless life and victory over death, we can rightly claim, through Christ, a glorious eternal life in His presence.

The story of the resurrection—the Son of God's victory over death—is impossible to express in words alone. It speaks to the heart and soul, as well as to the mind. That's why we are inviting you to be part of a celebration, to experience Easter more fully. We hope what you read in this little booklet will fill you with anticipation and inspire you to join us, as we explore the event that ensures the promise of eternal life.

The Easter service will take just an hour or two of your time. We hope you will come!

> God raised him from the dead, freeing him from the agony of death, because it was impossible for death to keep its hold on him.
>
> *Acts 2:24 NIV*

Though the resurrection of our Lord Jesus Christ is integral to the Christian faith, it is primarily celebrated with colored eggs, chocolate bunnies, and baskets of goodies. The true story, which includes the empty burial tomb, the burial clothes left behind, the angels' announcement, the mourners' sorrow transformed to ecstatic joy, Mary Magdalene's greeting, the encounters of the disciples, and Jesus' ascension from the Mount of Olives, is one of the most exciting stories ever told.

We plan to celebrate the resurrection with the fullest possible understanding of its implications for our present and future lives. We intend to explore how Jesus' victory over death has given us hope for eternal life.

Maybe you've never stopped to consider the why of the Easter season, or maybe you know and you've just lost touch with the magnificence of the event. Either way, the *why* is what brings Easter to life.

Hope came alive at Easter!

The resurrection story, recorded in the Bible in all four Gospels—Matthew, Mark, Luke, and John—is the foundation for the Easter celebration. If you decide to attend the Easter service, hearing the story ahead of time could greatly enhance your experience. The story begins with Jesus' cruel death on the cross and His burial.

Are you ready to come along with us as we take this incredible journey?

THE BURIAL OF JESUS

Matthew 27:57–66 NIV

As evening approached, there came a rich man from Arimathea, named Joseph, who had himself become a disciple of Jesus. Going to Pilate, he asked for Jesus' body, and Pilate ordered that it be given to him. Joseph took the body, wrapped it in a clean linen cloth, and placed it in his own new tomb that he had cut out of the rock. He rolled a big stone in front of the entrance to the tomb and went away. Mary Magdalene and the other Mary were sitting there opposite the tomb.

The next day, the one after Preparation Day, the chief priests and the Pharisees went to Pilate. "Sir," they said, "we remember that while he was still alive that deceiver said, 'After three days I will rise again.' So give the order for the tomb to be made secure until the third day. Otherwise, his disciples may come and steal the body and tell the people that he has been raised from the dead. This last deception will be worse than the first."

"Take a guard," Pilate answered. "Go, make the tomb as secure as you know how." So they went and made the tomb secure by putting a seal on the stone and posting the guard.

It must have seemed like the end of the world for the disciples of Jesus. They had tied all their hopes and dreams to the Teacher sent from God, looking to Him not only for spiritual understanding, but also for relief from the tyranny of the Roman occupation. Then they had watched as He was battered, mocked, and brutally murdered. Now, the only man who had ever given them hope was dead, left in the darkness of a borrowed tomb, and sealed in by order of the Roman government. Brokenhearted but still faithful, the women among Jesus' followers did all they could, preparing spices with which to embalm Jesus' body.

THE RESURRECTION

Luke 23:55–56; 24:1–12 NRSV

The women who had come with him from Galilee followed, and they saw the tomb and how his body was laid. Then they returned, and prepared spices and ointments. On the sabbath they rested according to the commandment.

But on the first day of the week, at early dawn, they came to the tomb, taking the spices that they had prepared. They found the stone rolled away from the tomb, but when they went in, they did not find the body. While they were perplexed about this, suddenly two men in dazzling clothes stood beside them. The women were terrified and bowed their faces to the ground, but the men said to them, "Why do you look for the living among the dead? He is not here, but has risen. Remember how he told you, while he was still in Galilee, that the Son of Man must be handed over to sinners, and be crucified, and on the third day rise again."

Then they remembered his words, and returning from the tomb, they told all this to the eleven and to all the rest. Now it was Mary Magdalene, Joanna, Mary the mother of James, and the other women with them who told this to the apostles. But these words seemed to them an idle tale, and they did not believe them. But Peter got up and ran to the tomb; stooping and looking in, he saw the linen cloths by themselves; then he went home, amazed at what had happened.

Sorrow gave way to surprise, and surprise gave way to amazement for these disciples of Jesus. Imagine going to mourn your loved one only to find Him gone without a trace. The women's minds must have been swimming and their hearts racing. And then two extraordinary men informed them that the person they were looking for had risen from the dead! Had not the past week been confusing enough?

It must have been bedlam when they arrived at the meeting place and told the others what they'd seen and heard. It was too much to believe for everyone but Peter. The memory he had of betraying his Master on the night of Jesus' trial must have caused him to hope against hope that he might somehow have an opportunity to see Jesus again and make things right. So with John right behind him, Peter ran to the tomb to see if Mary's story could possibly be true.

WHY DO YOU WEEP?

John 20:3–18 MSG

Peter and the other disciple left immediately for the tomb. They ran, neck and neck. The other disciple got to the tomb first, outrunning Peter. Stooping to look in, he saw the pieces of linen cloth lying there, but he didn't go in. Simon Peter arrived after him, entered the tomb, observed the linen cloths lying there, and the kerchief used to cover his head not lying with the linen cloths but separate, neatly folded by itself. Then the other disciple, the one who had gotten there first, went into the tomb, took one look at the evidence, and believed. No one yet knew from the Scripture that he [Jesus] had to rise from the dead. The disciples then went back home.

But Mary stood outside the tomb weeping. As she wept, she knelt to look into the tomb and saw two angels sitting there, dressed in white, one at the head, the other at the foot of where Jesus' body had been laid. They said to her, "Woman, why do you weep?"

"They took my Master," she said, "and I don't know where they put him." After she said this, she turned away and saw Jesus standing there. But she didn't recognize him.

Jesus spoke to her, "Woman, why do you weep? Who are you looking for?"

She, thinking that he was the gardener, said, "Mister, if you took him, tell me where you put him so I can care for him."

Jesus said, "Mary."

Turning to face him, she said in Hebrew, *"Rabboni!"* meaning "Teacher!"

Jesus said, "Don't cling to me, for I have not yet ascended to the Father. Go to my brothers and tell them, 'I ascend to my Father and your Father, my God and your God."

Mary Magdalene went, telling the news to the disciples: "I saw the Master!" And she told them everything he said to her.

Though Mary, a woman, was not counted among the Twelve—Jesus' disciples—she and Jesus were close. He considered her one of His own. He knew how deeply she loved Him and how confused and breathless she must have been at that moment. His words to her were gentle and caring.

TO BELIEVE

John 20:19–30 MSG

Later on that day, the disciples had gathered together, but, fearful of the Jews, had locked all the doors in the house. Jesus entered, stood among them, and said, "Peace to you." Then he showed them his hands and side.

The disciples, seeing the Master with their own eyes, were exuberant. Jesus repeated his greeting: "Peace to you. Just as the Father sent me, I send you."

Then he took a deep breath and breathed into them. "Receive the Holy Spirit," he said. "If you forgive someone's sins, they're gone for good. If you don't forgive sins, what are you going to do with them?"

But Thomas, sometimes called the Twin, one of the Twelve, was not with them when Jesus came. The other disciples told him, "We saw the Master."

But he said, "Unless I see the nail holes in his hands, put my finger in the nail holes, and stick my hand in his side, I won't believe it."

Eight days later, his disciples were again in the room. This time Thomas was with them. Jesus came through the locked doors, stood among them, and said, "Peace to you."

Then he focused his attention on Thomas. "Take your finger and examine my hands. Take your hand and stick it in my side. Don't be unbelieving. Believe."

Thomas said, "My Master! My God!"

Jesus said, "So, you believe because you've seen with your own eyes. Even better blessings are in store for those who believe without seeing."

Jesus provided far more God-revealing signs than are written down in this book. These are written down so you will believe that Jesus is the Messiah, the Son of God, and in the act of believing, have real and eternal life in the way he personally revealed it.

These were not the only times Jesus appeared to His disciples. He joined two of them as they walked along the road to Emmaus, about seven miles from Jerusalem. A few days later, He showed Himself again as Peter, Thomas, and Nathaniel fished on the Sea of Galilee. Just after daybreak, He stood on the shore and watched the weary fishermen pulling in empty nets. He called to them to throw out their nets on the right side of the boat, and when they did, their nets came up full almost to the point of breaking. After delivering their catch to shore, they found He had prepared breakfast for them. What emotions must have passed between them as they sat around the campfire and shared the bread and the fish.

Jesus' mission to die on behalf of all mankind and then rise again in triumph over death was complete when He rose up off the slab in the burial chamber. He could have simply returned to His Father, totally victorious. But Jesus was both Savior and Shepherd. He loved those who had walked with Him in His earthly life. He felt great compassion for what they had been through. He wanted to comfort them, assure them that no one had stolen His body, let them see for themselves that He had risen. And He wanted them to be able to bear witness to all those believers who would follow—witness that He was indeed alive! Death could not keep Him!

TO THE ENDS OF THE WORLD

Acts 1:3–12 MSG

After his death, he presented himself alive to them in many different settings over a period of forty days. In face-to-face meetings, he talked to them about things concerning the kingdom of God. As they met and ate meals together, he told them that they were on no account to leave Jerusalem but "must wait for what the Father promised: the promise you heard from me. John baptized in water; you will be baptized in the Holy Spirit. And soon."

When they were together for the last time, they asked, "Master, are you going to restore the kingdom to Israel now? Is this the time?"

He told them, "You don't get to know the time. Timing is the Father's business. What you'll get is the Holy Spirit. And when the Holy Spirit comes on you, you will be able to be my witnesses in Jerusalem, all over Judea and Samaria, even to the ends of the world."

These were his last words. As they watched, he was taken up and disappeared in a cloud. They stood there, staring into the empty sky. Suddenly two men appeared—in white robes! They said, "You Galileans!—why do you just stand here looking up at an empty sky? This very Jesus who was taken up from among you to heaven will come as certainly—and mysteriously—as he left."

So they left the mountain called Olives and returned to Jerusalem.

The disciples spent forty amazing days with their risen Lord while He taught them about the kingdom of God. Their hearts must have been emptied of fear and filled with joy. After all, the worst that could happen had happened, and here they were together again. And then, watching Him actually ascend into heaven—having seen that, they were fortified, ready for anything.

The future would prove difficult. They would be subjected to great persecution, beaten, and even martyred. But their faith would not fail. How could it? They had seen beyond the veil of this life and experienced a bit of eternity. And there was more. They would soon be empowered by the one Jesus called the Holy Spirit! They must have had difficulty containing their excitement as they walked back to Jerusalem and gathered together in an upper room to wait.

No doubt those gathered there had an amazing, life-altering experience. Even reading their eyewitness account brings renewed faith and strengthens our resolve to stand strong until He comes again.

It could be that you have been facing difficult times. Heartbreak, disappointment, and discouragement have weighed heavily on your heart. For a moment, imagine yourself face to face with the risen Lord, hearing Him speak, watching Him ascend into heaven. His great triumph changed everything for His disciples, and it can change everything for you, as well. Those who put their trust in Him went through some dark hours, but they were not disappointed.

Open your heart to Him. Speak to Him, for He is indeed alive and willing to listen to all you have to say. Trust in Him and you will find Him completely faithful.

God's Promise

Though the disciples clearly didn't comprehend what He was saying to them, Jesus did tell them, in advance of his death, what would happen to Him. He let them know that He would be betrayed, beaten, put on trial, and then crucified. And He included the promise that He would be raised from the dead. In *Matthew 16:21* we read that while He was still alive, Jesus assured His disciples He would rise from the dead: "Jesus began to show to His disciples that He must go to Jerusalem, and suffer many things from the elders and chief priests and scribes, and be killed, and be raised the third day" *(NKJV)*.

Many popular leaders have come and gone, but only Jesus was able to rise from the dead, just like He said He would. Only the tomb of Jesus is empty. Only the followers of Jesus have no burial place to visit. Only Jesus spoke with His disciples, ate with them, comforted them, and taught them—after His death.

Has God made promises to you? Jesus' resurrection demonstrates that He keeps His promises, and that's why you can be sure that He will keep all the promises He has made to you.

Who Was Jesus?

The primary purpose of the miracles recorded in the Bible was to confirm that a certain message or messenger had come from God. The resurrection of Jesus—the most substantiated of all Bible miracles—confirms that Jesus was and is who He claimed to be, the Son of God sent to pay the price for our sins. His victory over death proves He has the power to forgive, transform, and bestow the gift of eternal life on those who put their trust in Him.

When Jesus was born, the priest Simeon and the prophetess Anna knew who He was as they held Him in their arms, but for most, His true identity was revealed only over time. He was in fact the *Christ*, which means "the anointed one." *All human* and at the same time *all God*, Jesus was to serve as a go-between, a bridge between God and His creation. He had been sent to repair the broken relationship between God and man.

John, one of the eyewitnesses to Jesus' life and ministry, verifies Jesus' identity. However, the expression of this truth pushed John to the very limits of human language. He wrote, "In the beginning was the Word, and the Word was with God, and the Word was God," and "The Word became flesh and made his dwelling among us" *(John 1:1, 14 NIV)*. Jesus, the eternal *expression* ("Word") of God, had come to live in a human body. Jesus was both divine and human.

Finally! The promise of reconciliation between God and man was being fulfilled.

The book of Hebrews tells us that Jesus' death on the cross, some thirty-three years after His birth, fully satisfied the judgment for and made right the breach sin had caused. "Christ died once for all time as a sacrifice to take away the sins of many people. He will come again, not to deal with our sins, but to bring salvation to all who are eagerly waiting for him" *(Hebrews 9:28 NLT).*

During Jesus' life on earth, He taught us what it means to be fully human: to have a trusting, open, intimate relationship with God and with others. Jesus was not without His detractors. Eventually, Jesus' enemies succeeded in having Him put to death. They thought they were getting Him out of the way, but in truth they were playing right into God's plan. By surrendering His perfect life, Jesus revealed His role as our Messiah. He traded a perfect life for our lives, scarred and battered by sin. No longer were we identified as children of sin, but now children of God! Just as Adam and Eve walked with God in the garden of Eden, relishing His fellowship, all those who would accept Him were now wrapped, as it were, in His clean white robe and pronounced worthy to stand in His presence—loved and forgiven.

And having given His life, He rose from the grave and conquered the penalties for sin once and for all. No wonder the name *Jesus* means "savior." Hallelujah!

What one word best describes your relationship with God right now?

Do you find it interesting that God's plan for mending the breach in our relationship with Him involved the birth of a child? Yet what better way to bring us back into the family of God? As Jesus Himself put it, we can be *born again (John 3:3).* All of us were born once in a physical sense, and all of us need to be reborn spiritually in order to enter this new relationship with God.

We do that by *faith,* that is, by taking Jesus at His word and placing our confidence in Him. John the apostle said, "To all who did accept him and believe in him he gave the right to become children of God. They did not become his children in any human way—by any human parents or human desire. They were born of God" *(John 1:12–13 NCV).*

This is a profound change that goes far deeper than simply deciding to turn over a new leaf. When we accept the sacrifice

Jesus made for us on the cross, He sends His Holy Spirit to live within us. The result is that we are able to enter a trusting, honest, secure relationship with the One who created us.

Maybe you've already discovered who Jesus is. Maybe you've already made a decision to accept the sacrifice He made for you when He came to earth as a human being, lived a perfect life, and then died in your place on the cross so that you could be reunited with your heavenly Father. Maybe you already believe that God raised Him up on the third day! If you do, then you already know why Jesus' resurrection is so important to your life today.

A Gift for You

However, it's just as possible that you haven't until now fully understood what the events that transpired in that borrowed tomb mean for your life in the here and now. If that's the case, ask yourself, *Am I ready for a new sense of hope? A new beginning?*

The greatest gift any of us could hope to receive is the gift of new life that God has made possible through His Son, Jesus Christ. This new life is truly a gift. It isn't something you deserve or something you could earn. It's completely free.

Unlike those who had to wait so long for the fulfillment of God's promise, you can receive this gift today. The breach in your relationship with God, your Creator, has already been repaired. All you need to do is open the door of your heart and receive what God has prepared for you.

Listen with your heart and you will hear Jesus speaking to you right now. He is saying: "_____ [your name], *I came to earth so that you could become part of My family. I love you so much that I was willing to leave My heavenly throne, where I ruled alongside My Father, and take on the flesh-and-blood body of a human being. I then gave up My earthly life to pay the penalty for your sin and reconcile you with My Father.*

"Though My brief stay on earth was more than two thousand years ago, the work I did there is eternal. I was raised from the grave and am ever living. I continue to hold out My hand and invite you to accept the gift of My life. The moment you say yes to Me, you have a warm welcome into the family of God. In fact, you become an adopted son or daughter, and this adoption is complete

and final. I become not only your Savior, not only your Lord God, but also your brother, and My Father becomes your Father, as well.

"Regardless of what words you use, and no matter what difficulties your future may hold, you now can have joy for the rest of your life on earth, because My Holy Spirit will come to live in your heart. And when you die, the door to heaven will be wide open for you. I want nothing more than to spend eternity with you. My Father and I love you more than anybody on earth could possibly love you."

You can pray these words or use words of your own:

"Heavenly Father, I am aware of a separation from You, and I know that my sinfulness has gotten in the way. I believe now that Jesus Christ is Your Son, and that He came to earth as a human in order to take away the barrier of sin, including my own. I believe that when He suffered and died on the cross, He paid the full price of punishment for sin. I believe this means that I can be forgiven so that I can come into Your holy presence.

"I believe that You raised Jesus from the dead, proving that Your life is stronger than death, and that this opened the way to eternal life for me and for anyone who believes. With all of my heart, I want to start over; I want to be born again.

"I give my life to You, and I ask You to take full control of it. Of my own free will, I am making a decision to follow You, Jesus, and I thank You for inviting me to come into Your Father's family. I belong to You now. Amen."

The Bible makes it clear that those who accept Jesus Christ as their Lord and Savior will have all of their sins (past, present, and future) forgiven forever. Take a look at these confirmations from the Bible:

God so loved the world that He gave His only begotten Son, that whoever believes in Him should not perish but have everlasting life. For God did not send His Son into the world to condemn the world, but that the world through Him might be saved.
John 3:16–17 NKJV

Whoever believes in Him will receive remission of sins.
Acts 10:43 NKJV
He is so rich in kindness and grace that he purchased our freedom

with the blood of his Son and forgave our sins.
Ephesians 1:7 NLT

If we confess our sins, he is faithful and just and will forgive us our sins and purify us from all unrighteousness.
1 John 1:9 NIV

Praise the LORD, O my soul, and forget not all his benefits—who forgives all your sins… . as far as the east is from the west, so far has he removed our transgressions from us.
Psalm 103:2–3, 12 NIV

If you have just accepted Christ, you have something wonderful to celebrate. As is true with all family relationships, your relationship with God will grow stronger as you cultivate the love and trust that began today. Here are some simple things you can do to make that relationship grow:

First, tell someone about your decision to place your faith in Jesus. This will strengthen your desire to live in harmony with Him, and it will be your first opportunity to share the good news with someone else who is hungry for a relationship with God.

Next, begin the daily habit of talking with God through prayer. This can be done anywhere, anytime. Just talk with Him as you would with any person. As you pray and listen reflectively, you will sense God speaking with you too.

Also begin to feed your mind on the truth of God's Word, the Bible. You can find one at nearly any bookstore, or you can read it free on the Internet. Begin with one of the selections that tells about the life of Jesus, such as the Gospel of John.

Finally, gather with other believers for worship every week. This fellowship will greatly strengthen your faith, and you will be an encouragement to others, as well.

You are part of the family now, the family of God. Happy birthday!

Who is the first person you will tell about your new life with God?

Already a Believer

As we mentioned earlier, you may already be a member of the family of God. You may have known Jesus for a few years, many years, or even all of your life. No matter when you became a believer in the risen Savior, the glorious result is the same. You have been reconciled with God, your heavenly Father.

If you've been a Christian for a while, though, you may be reluctant to accept our invitation to the Easter service, not because you don't understand the significance it holds, but because you've had a bad experience with church in the past. It happens more often than any of us would like to admit. Just like with any big family, there is going to be conflict at times. In one of his many letters to first-century believers, the Apostle Paul wrote these words: "Be kind and compassionate to one another, forgiving each other, just as in Christ God forgave you" *(Ephesians 4:32 NIV).*

If there is one word that resonates throughout the Easter story, it is *reconciliation.* That involves relationship with God, but it also involves relationship with other Christians. It could be that attending church this Easter would be a good first step toward re-associating yourself with your brothers and sisters of faith.

Or it could be that your reluctance to go back to church is not nearly so complicated. It could be that you've just gotten busy, and now it's tough to fit church into your schedule. Don't worry; you are hardly the first person to drop out of church for lack of time. We live in a society that is always on the move. We spend our days rushing from one thing to another, trying to keep all the plates spinning and responsibilities covered. Many Americans are sleep deprived, emotionally depleted, and overwhelmed by responsibility. Church seems to be the easiest activity to drop. After all, God is forgiving, right? He isn't going to cut us off because we don't show up. That's true. But think about what is lost when you sacrifice church attendance to your crowded schedule:

1. You miss hearing the life-affirming Word of God read and discussed.
2. You miss the spiritual insights you can obtain from your brothers and sisters in the Lord.
3. You miss joining in with other believers as we praise and worship the Lord together.
4. You miss involving your family in church activities that will help them grow spiritually.
5. You miss the comfort of having a church family during difficult times.
6. You miss having fellowship with those who believe as you do.
7. You miss praying for the needs of others and having others to pray for your needs.
8. You miss sharing your blessings with others and rejoicing as they share their blessings with you.
9. You miss taking part as your local church reaches out to meet the needs of your community.
10. You miss knowing that your children are being nurtured in their relationships with God.

Suffice to say, you miss a lot. Doesn't it make sense to join us for our Easter service to remind yourself that church should be at the center of your life rather than on the outskirts?

The Bible makes it clear that going to church is an important part of the believer's life. Take a look at these confirmations from the Bible:

Let us not give up meeting together, as some are in the habit of doing, but let us encourage one another—and all the more as you see the Day approaching.

Hebrews 10:25 NIV

The body we're talking about is Christ's body of chosen people. Each of us finds our meaning and function as a part of his body.
　　　　　　　　　　　　　　　　　　　　　　　Romans 12:5 MSG

God's household .... is the church of the living God, the pillar and foundation of the truth.
　　　　　　　　　　　　　　　　　　　　　　　1 Timothy 3:15 NIV

COME ONE, COME ALL

Whether you are a new believer thinking about attending church for the first time or a seasoned believer thinking about going back to church, you may have some practical questions. Let's take a look at some church Q & A.

QUESTION:

What if I go to the Easter service and I feel invisible—no one talks to me?

Unfortunately, this happens sometimes in churches—even in our church. We human beings do tend to get caught up in our own circle of friends and family, and walking up and saying hi to someone new takes effort. But this Easter season, especially, we have made a commitment to open our eyes and ears and really see those around us. We have been praying for you, and that's the first step to successfully reaching out to those outside our familiar church family.

We also understand that we need you. Without new faces in the crowd, it would be easy to become ingrown and lose touch with the exciting things God is doing in the world.

We would also miss out on the special gifting God has placed in your life. It might be your warm smile, your ability to teach the Bible, your practical and spiritual insights, your lovely singing voice, your ability to play a musical instrument. It might be your gift for relating to the older members of our congregation or the younger. There are so many things to be done here in celebration of our renewed relationship with God, and we can't do it nearly as well without the gift that you contribute. The

Apostle Paul said it this way: "We have gifts that differ according to the grace given to us: prophecy, in proportion to faith; ministry, in ministering; the teacher, in teaching; the exhorter, in exhortation; the giver, in generosity; the leader, in diligence; the compassionate, in cheerfulness" *(Romans 12:6–8 NRSV)*. We need you as much as you need us! Come and let us prove it to you!

QUESTION:

What if I come to the Easter service but I'm not ready to commit to joining the church or even coming back for another visit?

We aren't asking for a lifelong commitment to attend our church. We would just love to have you come and be part of our Easter celebration, to worship with us as we commemorate the resurrection of our Lord and Savior. Of course, we are hopeful that you will come back to visit us again, and we will be delighted if you decide to come on a regular basis and get involved. But you don't need to worry. We won't be tracking you down and demanding to know where you've been. We just want a chance to love you and see if you could be happy here in our church body.

QUESTION:

If I choose *not* to come to church, does that make me a bad person?

Going to church is never about being good or bad. It's about the opportunity to grow in faith, to gain wisdom, to fellowship with people who appreciate mercy and compassion and forgiveness. It does, however, provide a vast array of opportunities to engage in good deeds. The whole purpose of church is to help you become more like Jesus, and He was certainly good. As you learn to live in right relationship with Him, the goodness in your own heart will shine through.

The point here is that church should be a positive influence in your life, a place where positive people do positive things. No one will judge you if you choose not to come, but they will keep encouraging you to come.

QUESTION:

If I *do* go to church, does that make me a good person?

Going to church can't make you good. That's God's work. Church is about helping you grow. Imagine taking a seed and putting it in soil and leaving it there. Will it grow? Probably—in fact, it may even develop into a small shrub with the help of rain, dew, and fresh air. But over time, the shrub will become stunted in its growth. The dead leaves and branches that dry out in the winter will start choking out new growth that wants to start in the spring. These new shoots have nowhere to go, so they will soon get so weak that they will shrivel and die.

What if that shrub had been tended by a gardener who clipped away its dead leaves, pruned its branches, and watered, fed, and nurtured it? The shrub would thrive and probably be in full flower every spring, constantly growing into a bigger and bigger masterpiece in the garden. Its roots would go down deep and spread wide, and it would be established and healthy. You may well be aware of some dead leaves and stunted growth in your own life. Maybe it's time to bring your shrub back to the gardener for some tending.

If you think this metaphor sounds familiar, it should. In this way, Jesus taught us about the importance of abiding (remaining) in Him. God is our gardener, Jesus is like the vine, and we are the branches. How can a branch sustain itself if it's not connected to the vine?

[Jesus replied:] "I am the true vine, and my Father is the gardener. He cuts off every branch in me that bears no fruit, while every branch that does bear fruit he prunes so that it will be even more fruitful. You are already clean because of the word I have spoken to you. Remain in me, and I will remain in you. No branch can bear fruit by itself; it must remain in the vine. Neither can you bear fruit unless you remain in me. I am the vine; you are the branches. If a man remains in me and I in him, he will bear much fruit; apart from me you can do nothing. If anyone does not remain in me, he is like a branch that is thrown away and withers;

such branches are picked up, thrown into the fire and burned. If you remain in me and my words remain in you, ask whatever you wish, and it will be given you."
(John 15:1–7 NIV)

QUESTION:

If I come for the Easter service, is someone going to pressure me to give money to the church?

Your concern is understandable. Churches are notorious for passing the offering plate up and down aisles filled with a captive audience. We don't mean to put pressure on you, though. The intention is just to provide for our church needs while providing an opportunity for you to give something to God and receive His blessing. We have learned that you can never out-give God. He always gives back so much more than we give to Him.

Just the same, we can assure you that taking an offering is not by any means the central priority when we gather to worship. That is especially true for the Easter service. You would be, first and foremost, our guest. Furthermore, we would never judge you for exercising your choice to give or not to give. So leave your wallet at home. We want you—not your money.

QUESTION:

What if the sermon is boring?

If you decide to join us for our Easter service, we guarantee it won't be boring! How could it be? How could the singing and the story of resurrection from the dead be boring?

We'll be honest, though. Should you choose to visit us regularly, you may not find every sermon to be as inspiring. For one thing, you may have limited understanding concerning the principles conveyed from the pulpit. You might not be familiar with the Bible characters or their situations. You might not be spiritually ready to digest all the preacher has to say.

What you may not know, however, is that this is a challenge for all of us. We've all come into this church at various levels of spiritual growth. Some of us learned the Bible stories in our childhood; others never entered a church building until we were grown. We've found that as we grow in our faith, we become more and more interested in what is being said by the preacher. For example, quantum physics is an amazing field, very exciting with its mind-bending theories and physical predictions. But individuals who have not studied the science might find it difficult to sit through a lecture on the subject. They would be unfamiliar with the terminology and the basic concepts that undergird the speaker's remarks. Only as they begin to learn and understand the science involved would their interest be piqued.

Of course, realistically, many of us will never be capable of learning about and enjoying such an advanced field of science. But God has guaranteed that all of us will be able to learn and master the principles of the Christian faith. When we become believers, the Holy Spirit comes into our hearts and minds and takes up residence. He is the One who helps us grow spiritually. He tutors us in our God understanding. In the Gospel of John, Jesus said to His followers: "The Counselor, the Holy Spirit, whom the Father will send in my name, will teach you all things and will remind you of everything I have said to you" *(John 14:26 NIV).*

We hope by now you've decided to accept our invitation to worship with us during our Easter service. But just in case you need more convincing, here are ten additional good reasons to come join us!

1. You remember Easter services from your childhood and would like to reconnect with those memories.
2. You would like to make the wonder and excitement of the Easter story a part of your annual Easter activities.
3. You want your children to hear the Easter story and be reminded that Easter is about more than egg hunts and chocolate bunnies.
4. You want to be with people during this season of celebration.
5. You want to be somewhere peaceful and holy as you meditate on the significance of this special time.
6. You enjoy singing the many uplifting songs that remind

you that you serve a risen Savior.
7. You've been thinking about going back to church anyway, and this would be a good time to do it.
8. You would like to get to know the person who gave you this booklet, and accepting his or her invitation would be the first step to doing that.
9. Being in church on Easter will remind you to keep your priorities in place.
10. You've been longing for a touch from God, and it seems like this would be a great time to reach out to Him.

We've done all we can to convince you to attend our Easter service. Even if you're sold, though, you may still have some practical concerns. Here are a few more questions we thought you might ask:

Question:

What should I wear?

We can assure you, it will not be necessary to go out and buy yourself something fancy to wear to our Easter service (or to any other service, for that matter). Sure, some people will dress up just because it is a custom for them to do so for this special occasion. If that's what you feel comfortable doing, feel free to add to the sense of pageantry for the day.

On the other hand, you may not be the type of person who likes to dress up, and that's quite all right too! Even for special services, it's acceptable to dress more casually and comfortably. No one will be calling the fashion police to complain about you or judging you for what you choose to wear. The only thing we ask is to dress modestly out of respect for the Lord.

QUESTION:

What time should I be there?

For the Easter service, it would be a good idea to get to the church fifteen or twenty minutes early to get a good seat, especially if you are coming with your family and loved ones. Coming too early might cause you to interrupt the choir or pageant rehearsal. And the greeters might not yet be in place to answer your questions or show you around.

If you decide to come back for a regular service, you should plan to be there about ten minutes early. This will give you time to drop off your children in the nursery, decide where in the sanctuary you are most comfortable sitting, and meet a few of your fellow churchgoers.

We hope you won't choose not to come because you're running a few minutes late or have to arrive after the service has started for some reason. The doors of our church remain open throughout the service, and you are welcome to join us at any time.

QUESTION:

Should I try to meet new people or just stay under the radar?

This is entirely your choice. Sometimes, it's less threatening to keep a low profile on the first visit. Simply be polite, and introduce yourself if asked. If someone asks if it's your first time, it's OK to tell the person that you're just visiting. Don't feel obliged to engage if you're not comfortable. Be open to meeting at least one new person, though. It will be easier to return if you can expect to see a familiar face.

One more thing: The Easter service is one of the times during the year when families tend to sit together. It's a great time to see who belongs to whom and make connections between parents and children, sisters and brothers, and even grandparents and their clans.

QUESTION:

Is there anything I need to bring?

If you have a Bible, bring it along so you can follow the Scriptures used in the sermon. But if you don't have a Bible, no worries. We have plenty, and we would be glad to share if you ask.

QUESTION:

How should I act?

All churches have their own ways of doing things, and this can seem scary at first when you're not sure what, when, or how to do these things. The best plan is to watch others around you. Regular attendees will know the routine, so follow their lead. If something seems weird or you don't understand it, just go with the flow. It will make sense eventually, and you can't be expected to know everything at first. You shouldn't feel obliged to participate in any aspect of the service that makes you uncomfortable, and it is OK to stay in your seat when others may stand up to sing or move to the front for prayer.

Remember your first day at a new school? You probably came that first day feeling a little insecure about what would be expected of you. But before long, you were well versed in how things were supposed to be done. Church protocol is no different. Of course, we'd like you to remember the usual courtesies like turning off your cell phone, keeping your voice low if you have to speak to someone, and letting us help you if your baby or small child is acting up. Other than that, there aren't any rules. We just want you to relax and enjoy yourself.

Question:

Should I respond to the request for follow-up information?

The Easter service may be an exception, but if you choose to visit us again, you may be asked to fill out an information card. We hope you won't feel intimidated by this. No one is going to knock on your door unannounced or ask you for money or obligate you in any other way. But wouldn't it be sad if you came and visited us and no one ever wrote down your name or had a record that you were there?

Just know that if you decide to come, it will mean a lot to us, and we will want to have an opportunity to introduce ourselves to you and find out a little about you. Sometimes, there isn't a chance for everyone to do that before or after the service. We want to do more than notice your face in the crowd. We want to remember you in our prayers and recognize your name if you should call for help sometime in the future. We want to be able to let you know when our congregation is doing something special that you might want to be part of. So ... no penalty for refusing to give us your information, but we hope you will.

The Most Important Tip of All

Be yourself! Come with an open heart and mind, and we are sure God will meet you here. We promise to do our best to make it a good experience for you, but there's no doubt what God will do. He will be waiting to bless you, comfort you, renew you, restore you, and fill you with joy. We hope this will be the very best Easter in your life so far. We pray that Jesus, the risen Christ, will become the central figure in your Easter story.

Until then, we hope you will be blessed by the words of this beloved Easter hymn, written by Charles Wesley!

Christ the Lord Is Risen Today

Christ the Lord is risen today, Alleluia!
Sons of men and angels say, Alleluia!
Raise your joys and triumphs high, Alleluia!
Sing, ye heavens, and earth reply, Alleluia!

Love's redeeming work is done, Alleluia!
Fought the fight, the battle won, Alleluia!
Death in vain forbids Him rise, Alleluia!
Christ hath opened Paradise. Alleluia!

Lives again our glorious King, Alleluia!
Where, O death, is now thy sting? Alleluia!
Dying once He all doth save, Alleluia!
Where thy victory, O grave? Alleluia!

Soar we now where Christ has led, Alleluia!
Following our exalted Head, Alleluia!
Made like Him, like Him we rise, Alleluia!
Ours the cross, the grave, the skies, Alleluia!